A pickle for the knowing ones, or, Plain truths in a homespun dress.

Timothy Dexter

A
PICKLE
FOR THE
KNOWING ONES:
OR
PLAIN TRUTHS
IN A
HOMESPUN DRESS.

By TIMOTHY DEXTER, Esq.

SALEM:
PRINTED FOR THE AUTHOR.
1802.

A Pickle for the Knowing Ones, &c.

TO mankind at Large the time is Com at Laſt the grat day of Regoiſing what is that whye I will tell you thous three kings is Raſed Raſed you meane ſhoued know Raſed on the firſt Royel Arch in the world olmoſt Not quite but very hiw up upon ſo thay are good mark to be ſcene ſo the womans Lik to ſee the frount and all peopel Loves to ſee them as the quakers will Com and peape ſlyly and feele glad and ſay houe the doue frind father Jorge waſheton is in the ſenter king Addoms at the Rite hand the preſent king at the Left hand father gorge wirh his hat on the other hats of the middel king with his ſword king Addoms with his Cane in a grand poſter Adteroude turning his faſs to wards the firſt king as if thay was on ſum politicks king our preſent king he is ſtands hearing being yonger and very deafe in ſhort being one graf féloſfer Looks well Eaſt & weſt and North & ſouth deafe & very deafe the god of Nater has dun very much for our preſent king and all our former ones thay are all good I want them to Live for Ever and I beleave thay will it is hard work to be A king — I ſay it is hardar then tilling the ground I know it is for I find it is hard work to be A Lord I dont deſier the ſound But to pleas the peopel at Large Let it gou to brak the way it dus for A fort ment to help A good Lafe to Cour the fick fpleney goutey dul frames Lik my felfe with the goute and fo on make merry a Chealy Chrifton is for me only be onneft No matter what thay worfhep fon moune or ftars or there wife or mifs if onneft Live for Ever money wont gitt thous figers fo faft as I wish I have fene to Leg horn for many mr bourr is one A-monks others I fent in the grand Crecham thous 3 kings Are plane white Leead colow at prefent the Rovel Arch & figers coft 39 pound wate filver the hieft Councaton order in the world fo it is fade by the knowing ones I have only 4 Lions & 1 Lam up the fpread Eagel hesbin up 3 years upon the Coupalay I have 13 billors front in ftrat Row for 13 ftates when we begun 3 in the Rear 15 foot hie 4 more on the grafs fee 2 the fame hath at the Rite of the grand Arch 2 at the left wing 15 foot hie the Arch 17 foot hie the my hous is 3 forey upwards of 290 feet Round the hous Nater has formed the ground Eaquel to what you would wifh for the Art by man Eaquel to A Sol-omun the onerbel Jonathan Jackfon one of the firft in this Conntry for taft borne A grat man by Nater then the beft of Lurning what fot me fored for my plan having fo gran fpot the hool of the world Cant Excead this to thous that dont know would think I was Like halfe the world A Lier I have traveled good deale but old fteady men fayeth it is the firft that it is the firft beft in this Contry & others Contrey I tell you this the trouth that None of you all great men wodent be A frunted at my prefeadens & I fpare Now Coft in the work I have ahe tempel of Reafon in my garding 3 years paft with a toume under it on the Eage of the grafs fee it coft 98 gineys befids the Coffen panted whit in fide & out fide tuched with green Nobel trimings uncommon Lock fo I can tak the kee in fide and have her works in the toume pipes & tobacker & A fpeaking trumpet and A bibel to Read & fum good fongs.

What is a prefedent anfwer A king bonne partey the grat has as much power as A king and ort to have & it is a maffey he has for the good of mankind he has as much power as Any king for grat ways back there mnft be A head fum whare or the peopel is Loft Lik wild gees when thay Lous the head gander two Leged wants A head if fore Leged both & 2 Leged fouls the Name of prefedent is to pleafe the peopel at Large the found fouts beft Now in the fouth give way the North the North give way to the fouth or by & by you will brake what fulers be wife on keep the Links to gether and if you cant A gree Confoalated to A kingly power for you muft keep to gether at the woft hear it Labers ye les fee there is fo many men wants be the all offefers & Now fogers poor king Every day wants A bone fum more then others the king cant Live without the feald wee have had our turne grat good father Addoms turne & turne A bout Reft Ealey you all will be pleafed with the prefent king give time all did I fay Now but the magor part fore fifths at leaft

TIMOTHY DEXTER

FRINDS hear me 2 granadears gofs up in 20 days fourder frinds I will tell the A tipe of man kind what is that 35 or 36 years gone A town caled Noubry all won the Younited ftates Noubry peopel kept to gether quiet till the Larned groed ftrong the the farmers was 12 out of 20 thay wanted to have the offesers in the Contrey the Laned in the see port wanted to have them there geering A Rofe groued worme fite thay wood in Law thay went the Jnrel Cort to be fot of finely thay got there Eands Anfwered the fee port caled Newbury Port 600 Eakers of Land out of thirty thoufand Eakers of good Land to much for mad peopel of Larning makes them mad if thay had kept to gether thay wood have bin the fekent town in this ftat A bout halfe of boston Now men mad to be in offefs it hurts the peopel at Large Like Carying the Innegent Lam to flarter Now it would doue to dewide the North from the fouth all won what I have Leade down but Now keep to gether it is Like man and wife in troue Love Now guving death in the grander you will fous the glory I fay keep to gether dont brak the Chane Renoue brotherle Love Never fade Like my box in my garding be one grat famiey give way to one A Nother thous changes is the tide hie warter & Loue warter hie tids & Loue tids for my part I have Liked all the kings all three all our broken marchants cant have beaths of proffett goue and till the gronnd goue to work is all that has bin to Coleage goue with flipers and prom's to pay and Never pay onty wi h A Lye I gets 4 fifths is Coleage Lint or devel Lant or pretended to be onneft free mafions but are to the Contry for give me for gefling I hope it is Not fo the Leaned is for Leovs & Littel fifhes mofes was but A man and Aaron thay had fum devel Like my felfe man is the fame give him power I fay the Cloak Cukement made's the waft of cheats we hant got any N Port wee are Noted to be the firft in the North fabed Day is Not halfe A Nuf Night meatens it maks work for the

Dockters and Nufes Ceaching Could but them that Lives breed faft to mak up for them that dies poor creaters I pittey them fo preaft Riden it is wickard to leave poor fols in to the grave all our mineftere are imported Very good men foull of Love of Crift I kep them A mit Amen at prefent.

THE yong man that doth moft all my Carving his work is much Liked by our grat men I felt founney one day I thort I would afk fade young man whare he was bone. he fade Now whare what is all that Now whare was your mother over fhaderd I fays my mother was if I was to gefs No I tell in Now town borne o on the water I fays you beat me and fo wee Lafed and it fhuk of the fpleane fhoue him A Crows Neaft he can carve one A fine fellow—I fhold had all marbel if any bodey could to me the prife fo I have fent for 8 bufts for kings and grat men and 1 Lion & 2 gray hounds I hope to hear in foue Days to all onneft men

TIMOTHY DEXTER

mifter printter I muft gou fum fouder I have got one good pen my fortin has bin hard very hard that is I have had hard Noks on my head 4 difrent times from A boy to this Day twice taken up for dead two beatings was a Lawyer then he put me blind 7 days 2 tockters he was mad be Cafe the peopel at Large Declared me Lord Dexter king of Chefter this at my Contrey feet 26 mils from N Port my plafe there is the fift from folt water to Canedey——this Lawyer that broufed me was Judg Livemore fon Arther the fame Creater borid 200 dolors fum monts be fore this

& then Oaded me he beat his bene facter it has bin my Luck to be yoused ten times wos by them I doue the most for I have Lost first and Last as much as A tun of silver grose my wife that was had 400 wut of silver Abraham bishup that maried my dafter ten years gone him & shee sence then & my son Samuel L Dexter upwards seventeene thousands Dolors the Rest by hamsher Col by Rougs has gokbey sekkent handed preasts Deakens gruntiers whimers Every foue minnets A sith or Christ wee must be Leave in Crist o o Jeases will save us I thinks sum times the saving solt & smoak & solt peater will in time be very dear if it is yous the more smoak or the preasts will be out of work Littel Like sister france I Lade out A blan to have holerdeys one Day in ten 24 years gone I thort it would save the Natision grat Deale of money *sir* in one sentrey then the preasts wood have time to studdery then I amer Down smartly make the sulffer smoak in their Nostels under the Cloak of bread & wine the hipecricks Cloven foots thay Doue it to git power to Lie and Not be mistruested all wars mostly by the suf the broken marchents are fond of war for thay hant Nothing to Lous & the minesters in all wars the Cafe o god Leave the Divel out when it is all Divel If you can bare the trouth I will tell the trouth man is the best Annemel and the worst all men are more or Less the Divel but there is sit of ods sum halfe sum three qurters the other part beast of Difrent kind of beasts sum one thing and sum a Nother sum Like a Dog sum Lik horses sum bare s Cat sum Lion sum lik ouls sum a monkey sum wild Cat sum Lam sum A Dove sum a hogg sum a oxe sum a snake I want Desepons to be Dun A way but thay wont Never be as Long as prist

Riden what Doue the preaſt prech to the Divel for all there hearaes old & youn more or Leſs the Divel I Liked to fade fo Divel preaches to Divels Rebouking fin keep it up up up fayeth the hipacrits mockers of god habits an Coſtom is the ods ods maks the difrence fees god in all plafes the god of Nater in all things wee Live and move in god he is the god of Nateer all Nater is god take one Ellement from us one of the fore ake the fier or the water or or Eare or Earth wee are gone fo wee Live in god Now Lefs us all be good children doue all things Rite the ſtrong muſt bare the Infiemiteys of the wickead fhildren keep up the Laws Draw the Ranes Littel harder ſtop theavs as faſt as you can bad trade fheuuing Nine Numbers was Rot in 23 owers when I had hold of the pen five houers & 35 minnets A fort ment A fort ment is good in A fhop———

the preaſts fixes there goods fix days then thay open fhop on fundays to fell there goods fum fets them of better then others bolerhed when a man is fo week he wont doue for A Lawyer mak a preaſt of him for week thing to goue with week things the blind to Lead the blind fo thay may fall into one Dich and fo thay goue throue the world darkinefs but foue peopel have A pinon of there one Not one in twenty as to this world goods and fo it is as to the other world to Inquire the way goue to a fryer our peopel a bout the fame only call it fumthing Efe in Rum of a king call it diefedent but preaſts have money to fave fols I want to know what a fole is I wifh to fee one Not a gizard, I thinks the fole is the thinking part there is grat minds & Littel minds grat fols & Littel fols grat minns & littel minds According to the hevdey bod:

B

deys that has the power of our boddeys the same mother and the same father and six children how thay will differ in Looks complexions and axons sum for grat thing sum for littel things sumthing Nouw I say I say my figers will pay Intress money prove it first going over my brige sum more tole then helping the markett of the town Leeting hoses taven keepers costom the honner to the town & my selfe
TIMOTHY DEXTER.
one thing fourder I have bin convarted upwards 30 years quite Refsned for the day the grat day I wish the preast Node as much as I think I doue there harts would Leap up to glory to be so Reader for the time of Regoising to goue to be maried to what a fine widdow with hur Lamp bourning the Lamps trimed with glorey the shaking quickers after they git convarted and there sins washed A way thay stay at home & Let thous goue unclene and so it is much so with me I stay, at home praying for theavs and Rougs to be saved Day and Night praying for siners poour creaters my hous keeper is in the dark wos then bid Crasey to be saved shee says shee has sind A ganst the holey gost I have Asked her what is shee says it is sumthing but cant find out way sends for the preast coms what is the mater gost gost Dear sir & the minester makes a prayer the gost went of mostly not all part stayed behind shee has bin crasey Ever sence the preast cant Lay the serpont houe many Nick Names three things have so sayeth the preacher Amen Amen see sath I du

---

Noue mister printer *sir* I was at Noue haven 7 years and seven monts past at commencent Degrees

going on 40 boys was tuck degrees to doue good or
Not good the old man with the hat on told them to
fuedey houeman Nater & walk as A band of brothers
from that time to this day I thort that all thous that
was brot up to Coleage the meaning was to git there
Liveing out of the Labeer If the Coleages was to
continer one fentrey & keep up the game recken the
coft of all from there cradel to 22 years old all there
fathers and gurdEands to Lay out one houndred years
intrefs & intrefs upon intrefs gefs at it & caft it fee
houe many houndred thoufand millons of Dolors it
would com to to mak Rougs and theaves to plunder
the Labering man that fweats to git his bread good
common Laning is the beft fum good books is beft
well under ftoud be onneft dont be preaft Riden it is
a cheat all be onneft in all things Now feare Let this
goue as you find it my way fpeling houe is the ftrang-
eft man   T DEXTER

fourder mifter printer for A minefter to git the tone
is a grat pint when I lived in hamfher one Noue Lit
babftis babler fobed A way juft finefhing his fermon he
fays o good Lord I hop you will confider what foue
hints I have given and I will cleare it up fum time
hence I am much wore down Now the wether being
very worme to day Lefs bray & fo went on fire fire
& brimftone & grunting & fithing and tryed to cry
& fnufel & blow the fconks horne & fum the old
fouls & yong fouls fot to crying I tuck my hat and
went out houe mankind & women kind is in pofed
upon all over the world more or lefs by preaft craft o
for fhame o for fhame I pittey them be onneft doue as
you would wifh others to doue unto you in all things
Now fear of Death, A men   T D'a

fourder what difrent wous wee have of this world & the other world two good women Lived in A town whare I once lived one was sick of a consumson Near Death both belonged to the Church very onnest only the well woman was week in wous & thing says unto the sik woman I thinks you will see my housbon doue tell him I and my son A greus very well and wee are all well and the sow is piged and got seaven pinney pigs and sare you well sister this I beleave is setting troue & so fare the well—I shall com A gane in Littel while

and sourdermore I am for sum soue Decephons but very foue souer then Deathe preast craft is very good for what to make old women fart and yong children cry and old fouls sling snot o yess and brak up familey Doun by untrouths Lying and swaring to A Lye stop I am a Live old me I have heard your wickard stuf you have ingerd my srinds a plenty and if you dont stop I will call forth one Abraham bishup to put Niklos and all that trys to keep up Lving if there should be any such stuf in the Land Church members pant to be fonnd of Desepchon thay are parfect but if there is any put them with the tufe bourne the Roubege piss on it or that feare Not wind or filth go by the Rackel breed and was then turde I Like to sade Now shitt skink strong bread & wine boue is bread & wne master boull houe is the boull a black man a frind to John mekel jentel man from A Crows Nect Whare Now whare ass Cole cole ass whare whare Now whare o yess sum whare deare oilen Now the Ingons Lived there onle that Cant be he was from hell whare his or was brother came from oyes oyes o yes A Crows Neast or ergen pouler Down

FROM THE MUSEUM OF

TIMOTHY DEXTER, Esq.

IME the first Lord in the younited States of A mercary Now of Newburyport it is the voise of the peopel and I cant Help it and so Let it goue Now as I must be Lord there will foler many more Lords prittey soune for it Dont hurt A Cat Nor the mouse Nor the son Nor the water Nor the Eare then goue on all is Easey Now bons broaken all is well all in Love Now I be gin to Lay the Corner ston and the kee ston with grat Remenbrence of my father Jorge Washington the grate herow 17 sentreys past before we found so good A father to his shildren and Now gone to Rest Now to shoue my Love to my father and gaate Caracters I will shoue the world one of the grate Wonders of the world in 15 months if now man mourders me in Dors or out Dors such A mouserum on Earth will annonce O Lord thou knowest to be troue sourder hear me good Lord I am A goueing to Let or shildren know Now to see good Lord what has bin in the world grat wase back to owr fore fathers Not old plimeth but stop to Addom & Eave to shoue 4,5 figers two Leged and sore Leged b-cose we Cant Doue weel with out sore Legd in the first plase they are our soude in the Next plase to make out Dexters mouseum I wants 4 Lions to defend thous grat and mistiy men from East to wist from North to South which Now are at the plases Rased the Lam is Not Readey in short meater if Agreabel I forme A good and pealabel gov̇ement on my Land in Newburyport Compleat I taks 3 presedents hansher govener all to Noue york and the grate mister John Jay is one, that maks 2 in that ſtate the king of grat britton miſter pitt Rouſus king Croſs over to france Loues the 16 and then the grate bonnepartey the grate and there ſegnetoure Crow biddey——I Command peaſe and the grateſt brotherly Love and Not fade be Linked to gether with that beſt of troue Love ſo as to govern all naſions on the faſs of the gloub not to tiranize over them but to put them to order if any Deſpout ſhall A Riſe as to boundreys or Any maturs of Importence it is Left france and grat britton and Amacarey to be ſetteled A Congreſs to be allways in france all Deſpouts is to be thare ſetteled and this may be Dun this will balleſs power and then all wars Dun A way there-fore I have the Lam to Lay Dow with the Lion Now this may be Dun if thos three powers would A geray to Lay what is called Devel one ſide and Not Carry the gentelman pack hors Any longer but ſhake him of as duſt on your feet and Laff at him; there is grate noiſe Aboute a toue Leged Creter he ſays I am going to ſet ſade black Divel there, ſtop he would ſcare the womans ſo there would be No youſe for the bilding, I ſhould have to E rect ſum Noue won, Now I ſtop hear, I puts the Devil Long with the bull for he is a bulling 2 Leged Annemal ſtop put him one ſide Near Soloman, Looking with Soloman to Ladey venus Now ſtop wind up, there is grat ods in ſtoute I will Let you know the ſekret houe you may ſee the Devel, ſtand on your head before a Loucking glaſs and take a bibel in to your bouſum faſt 40 owers and look in the loucking glaſs, there is no Devil if you dont ſee the ould fellow. but I affirm you will ſee that old Devel :

Unto you all mankind Com to my hous to mock and ſneare why ye Dont you Laſe be fore god or I meane your betters think the heir power Dont know thorts and Axſions Now I will tell you good and bad it is Not pelite to Com to ſee what the bare walls keep of my ground if you are gentel men you would ſtay Away when all is Dun in marble I Expect to goue out my ſelfe to Help it thous grat men will ſend on there Likeneſs all over the younited States I wiſh all the printers would ſend on there Likeneſes in 40 Days to Timothy Dexter I mean I want the printers to give Notis if pleaſes to in form by printen in the Nouſpapers for the good of the holl of man kind ———

I wans to make my Enemys grin in time Lik A Cat over A hot puding and goue Away and hang there heads Doun Like A Dogg bin After ſheep gilty ſtop ſee I am Afrade I Rite toue haſh my peopel Complane of backker ſpittel maks work to Cleane it up——in the women ſkouls A bout it ſpit in ther hankerſhif or not ſpit A tall I muſt ſay ſumthing or I ſhould ſay Nothing there fore make ſum Noiſe in the world when I git to ouely to Naſh my goms and griſing for water and that is ſalt water when brot A young Devel to bring it and A Scoyer to wate and tend on gentelmen A black Suter his breth Smelt wos then bram ſtone by far but Let the Devel goue in to Darknes and take his due to Delcare mankind for A Littel while this Cloven foot is ſeen by ſum but the trap will over hall the Devel in tim, I pittey this poore black man I thinc his maſter wants purging A Littel to har ber mr Devel A moſt but I did Not ſay Let him Run A way good Nit mr Devel Cary the ſword and money with you tak John mekel Jentel man good Nit

T DEXTER.

THIS COMETH GREETING

mister prin'ers the Igrent or the Nowings wons says I ort to Doue as thay Doue to keep up Cheats of the same thing Delephons to Deseave the Igrent so wee may Cheat and Likewise have wars and plunder my wish is all Liers may have there part of fier and brimstone in this world or at least sum part part of it or Else the gouement is Not good it will want pourging soone if A Lawyer is to way Lay a man an brouse him unmassely All most to Death A sitteson that pays twentey sore Dolors for Careags and more then one Dolor A week to ment the hiways and my being Libperel is in part of this bloddey Asare No sauage would beat a man as I was beaten almost to Death I Did not know houe these men Came to keep sade Lawyer from quit kilirg of me till sum time After three men saw the Axon of the blodey seene without massey and carried sade Dexter in to the house sun santing or Neare to it se and behold the olful site bleading and blind of one Eye twoue brousings in two hours at Least New Laws in this part of the world Now part of the world for A man of money to Live those I lend money to and A Lawyer and others thay youse me the wost it maks Inemye then those Rogs if there is Any that call me A soull and pick A Qualrel with me A bout my Nous papers so as to pay the Lawyer Craft to make up the molton Calf A molton Calfe Not an Ox Now the town of Chester has Lost two *hundred wate of Silver* at Least I beleuv more money Now thay may have me in the town or A Lawyer Chouse for yourselves my frinds and felow mortels pease be with you All A men selagh finely brethren sum thirg more Coming——— TIMOTHY DEXTER.

Chester, Sept. 29, 1796.

[17]

I say to houme it may confarne Now to our Rulers for a hearing in the firſt plafe Dexter and others confarned in the firſt brigge on the merremak it has payed to the town of N Port and Cuntry at large twenty per fent, one thirde to each party, the owners one third of twenty per fent. This is worrey of prafe fenfe this brigge was finifhed two more briges has been done over A bove on the fame River. the Rocks brige is a waft of money and Laber if there was no Rocks brigg the havrel brigg would barly pay the undertakers in bilding fade brigg Now no onneſt men can burne at the hart with gruging the proffetts of any one of thous brigges. The Rocks brigg is moſt dun the money is Loſt havvrel brigg barly pays the way when the Rocks brigg is Dun and Now more Dexters brigg and others oners doue but have halfe fo much Intreſt as bankers the Repars & & & fo on has bin grate to finifh the Repars back and fored to next ougeſt is five thoufand dolars in nine or ten years or there A bouts and you all know how money has bin fum part of the time very bad in worth

the town of N Port is likely to grow in thirty years to Doubel be twelve thoufand peopel three thoufand A bove this brigg talked of

No 2 further pleafe your honours, there is A bout Eight hundred Rodd in lenth to the Deare Oilen brigg & one hundred Rod in weth to bring it fquare Nobel houfe Lotts Number of bilding yards up to this Deare Oilen Brigg and many plafes for warfes Nater has formed N Port and part of Noubry as well for peafe and war all together as well as the Lord would wifh to have it and now lett us be wife in proving in proving

C

it in peaefe and godly love Not gruging one Another if fixty three oners was now as at firft in Dear oflen brigg this hart ourning wodent be fot on fier Now but twenty five oners fuch and fuch paffons feels hurt pretending there is toue much profets to Dexter in petickler he has twelve per fent grate meftake they choufe to Lye to hurt me becofe it is the moft of my bread the beft Anker to my fhip I have bought at fifty pounds A fhare in twelve monts paft, people has offen afked me why I did not bye the holl I have offen told them mankind was mankind it wod not doue nor wod it doue for a foue people to hold all the public feccoureteys for mankind was fo much of what wee Call the Devel or Roaring Lions or wouls.

No 3 fourder there is plenty of Complant of the difficulty of pafing thofe briges Now as it is troue if thofe giddy people have Liberty to bould A brigg it wont pay but three or four per fent at moft then thay muft have one haife the paffing of my brigg as I call it A mad bifnefs Now as for A turn pik from Newbrey brige to Epffwith is not bad it may doue middling well fix one way half a Dozen tother way & from Epffwith to beble brigg and fo on to Bofton Amen or from Dexters brige to moulden brigg or Reather to Noue bofton brigg it may have its wate as much as Ever wee ant Ripe for fo many grate things wate feven years Longrer time

I fay wate twelve years before you have Any more briges within four miles of meremack brigg I have it in contemplafion to give twenty five fhares to the town of N. Port to be kept at there expence in Repais the Incom for mending ftreets in the town of N. Port for that fole yous to be fixed in my laft will----well Dun

I meane this After 12 years for the town of N Port to hav twenty five shars from march first day one thousand Eigh hundred and two to be in foull forse and power greeting I ones one hundred ten shars there is two hundred in the holl the first Cost and Repars is A bout forty thousand and seven hundred Dollars

I am a frind to all onnest men

TIMOTHY DEXTER.

NOW WONDER.

T. DEXTER says four things—Wants good judgment to live in the world, in *giving* and *lending*, *trusting* and *borrowing*. For I begin to see I have already given my wife, that *was*, and my son Samuel L. Dexter, and Bishop, more than ten thousand dollars, in two years, and neither of them thank me. Now to all men that owes me, be so kind to themselves and me, as to pay me in a very short time, or else call and pay squire Bradbury's son the lawyer in *Newburyport*, without further trouble and cost.

TIMOTHY DEXTER.

FOR THE IMPARTIAL HERALD.

Messrs. BLUNT and MARCH,

I say to whom it may concern—to the majesty of the people of Newburyport, Greeting—

It costs Eight hundred Dollars a year to support a watch in this town, and yet gentlemen's windows are broken, fences pulled down and Cellars broken open, and much other misdemeanors done at night. Are the watch asleep, or are they afraid to detect those who are guilty of such practises? Boast not of it, if you call this Liberty and Equality. Newburyport has had the name of being a very civil worthy place; it is a great pity some bad boys or young men should disgrace it. I hope our worthy and honorable rulers will bring those rude lads to see themselves, and lick the dust like serpents, and ask forgiveness of their betters, and do so no more, but repent and live.

Now fellow citizens is it wisdom, is it policy, to use a man or men so shocking bad as to oblige them to leave the town where they paid one Dollar a day to support government?

A friend to good order, honor to whom it belongs, to great men a friend—to all good citizens and honest men good bye.

WHEREAS many philosophers has judged or guessed at many things about the world, and so on. Now I suppose I may guess as it is guessing times. I guess the world is one very large living creature, and always was and always will be without any end from everlasting to everlasting, and no end. What grows on this large creature is trees and many other things. In the room of hair the rocks is moulds. This is called land where the hair grows, the belly the sea—all kinds of fish is the worms in the belly. This large body wants dressing to get our living of this creature and by industry we get a living—We and all the animal creation is less than fleas in comparison on the back or belly of this very large immense body. Among the hairs to work this great body is that of nature, past finding out.—All we know is we are here, we come into the world crying and gone out groaning. Mankind is the master beast on the earth—in the sea, the whale is the head fish—the great fish eat up the little ones, and so men not only destroy one another, but they are master over the whole of beasts and fish, even over a lion, therefore men is the masterly beast, and the worst of the whole—they know the most and act the worst according to what they know. Seeing mankind so bad by nature, I think when the candle goes out, men and women is done, they will lay as dirt or rocks till the great gun fires, and when that goes off the gun will be so large that the gun will contain nine hundred million tons of the best of good powder, then that will shake and bring all the bones together, then the world will be to an end. All kind of music will be going on, funding systems will be laid aside, the melody will be very great. Now why can't you all believe the above written as well as many other things to be true, as well as what was set forth in the last Centinel concerning digging up a frog twenty feet below the surface, where it was most as hard as a rock—there was his shape like taking a stone out of a rock—This is from a minister. Now why wont you believe me as well.

WONDER OF WONDERS!

How great the soul is! Do not you all wonder and admire to see and behold and hear? Can you all believe half the truth and admire to hear the wonders how great the soul is—only behold—past finding out! Only see how large the soul is!—that if a man is drowned in the sea, what a great bubble comes up out of the top of the water!—the last of the man dying under water—this is wind—is the soul that is the last to ascend out of the deep to glory—it is the breath from on high doth go on high to glory. The bubble is the soul. A young fellow's for gunning for the good of bodies and souls.

APPENDIX.

The follering peases are not my Riting but very drole   TIMOTHY DEXTER.

Mr. Melcher,
Your publishing the following extract from a letter said to be from a trader among the Indians to a friend, may amuse some of your customers for the Gazette.

A few days ago one of the Indians paid me a visit, after some conversation, he said that a minister from the United States had been with his tribe to teach the Christian religion. He says that there is but one only living and true God, who is a good, wise, and powerful spirit (this Indian say too) and that there are three persons in the godhead, of one substance and power, God the Father, God the Son, and God the Holy Ghost, that the Father is of none neither begotten, or proceeding, the Son is eternally begotten of the Father, the Holy Ghost eternally proceeding from the Father and the Son, and that the Holy Ghost visited a Virgin, and conveyed the Son into her; where he continued nine moons and then was born like other children, was born God and man, that when he was about thirty years old began to preach, but the great men no like his preaching, sent their warriors who took and killed him.

Indians ask what all this talk mean. he say that the first man and woman broke God's law in eating fruit which God had forbidden, that therefore they and all the children that should proceed from them must die, and be punished after death forever, that the son came and died to save some of mankind from being punished after death—Oh! 'trange that man could kill God the Son, and that his death be of service to mankind---great many people die before the Son of God, and did not know any thing about him—it was then asked whether his dying would do poor indians any good, he say yes, if they believe, then me say that pappufe no believe them do them no good; he say you must leave that with God, and believe for yourself—one say it is hard to believe such 'tories; if Indian tell such 'trange things, the white people no believe um.

―――――

A curious Sermon, by the Rev. Mr. Hyberdin; which he made at the request of certain thieves that robbed him on a hill near Harrisrow, in Hampshire, (England) in their presence and at that instant.

I Greatly marvel that any man will difgrace thieving, and think that the doers thereof are worthy of death, confidering it is a thing that cometh near unto virtue, being used in all countries, and allowed by God himfelf; the which thing I cannot compendiously show unto you at so short a warning, and on so sharp an occasion. I must desire you, gentle audience of thieves, to take in good part what at this time cometh into my mind not doubting but that you, thro your good knowledge, are able to add much more unto it than this which I shall now offer unto you

First, Fortitude and stoutness of courage, and also boldness of mind, is commended of some men to be a virtue; which being granted, who is there then that will not judge thieves to be virtuous? For they are, of all men the most stout and hardy, and the most void of fear; for thieving is a thing usual among all men; for not only you that are here present, but also many others in divers places, both men, women and children, rich and poor, are daily of the faculty, as the hangman at Newgate can testify; and that it is allowed of by God himself is evident from scripture: For if you examine the whole course of the Bible you will find that thieves have been beloved of God; for Jacob when he came out of Mesopotamia, did steal his uncle Laban's kids. The same Jacob also stole his brother Esau's blessing and yet God said, *I have chosen Jacob and refused Esau.* The children of Israel, when they came out of Egypt, did steal the Egyptians' jewels of silver and jewels of gold, as God commanded them to do.

David in the days of Abiathar, the high priest, came into the temple and stole the hallowed bread; and yet God said, "David is a man after my own heart." Christ himself, when he was here on earth, did take an ass and a colt that was none of his; and yet God said, "This is my beloved son in whom I am well pleased." *That you see that God delighted in thieves.*

But most of all I marvel that men can despise thieves whereas in many points you be like Christ himself; for Christ had no dwelling place no more than you—Christ at length was caught, and so will you—he went into hell, and so will you.—In this you differ from him, for he rose and went into heaven—so you will never do without God's great mercy, which God grant you. To whom with the Father, Son, and Holy Ghost, be all honor and glory, for ever and ever. AMEN.

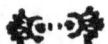

CPSIA information can be obtained
at www.ICGtesting.com
Printed in the USA
BVHW012001150922
647149BV00008B/72